STARTERS
LONG AGO
BOOKS

How
Writing Began

Macdonald Educational

This cave man is painting pictures
on the wall of his cave.
Cavemen used pictures to tell stories
and leave messages.

2

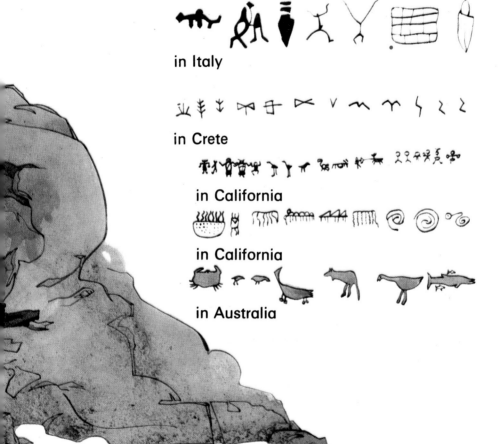

in Spain

in Italy

in Crete

in California

in California

in Australia

Here are some more old pictures.
They are called petroglyphs.
Pictures like this can be found
in many parts of the world.
They were the first kind of writing.

3

This man is sending a message.
He is carving it on wood.
This is how men sent messages
on Easter Island long ago.

4

Here is an Aztec book.
The Aztecs lived in Mexico long ago.
The book told the story
of a man called Eight-Deer.

5

stone

clay

People used to write on all kinds of things.
Some people carved on stone.
Others made marks in clay.

6

wax
tablet

Here are some Roman schoolboys
writing on wax tablets.
They make deep lines in the wax.

7

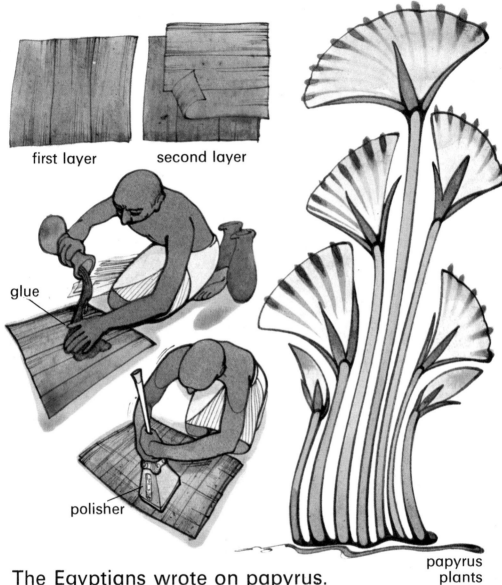

first layer

second layer

glue

polisher

papyrus plants

The Egyptians wrote on papyrus.
Papyrus is a reed.
They sliced the reeds and wove them
into a kind of paper.

8

Chinese paper

The Chinese made the first real paper.
They made it from linen rags.

9

obelisk

The Egyptians left many things
for us to read.
This obelisk shows their picture writing.
Each picture stands for a word.
This was the first kind of Egyptian writing.

10

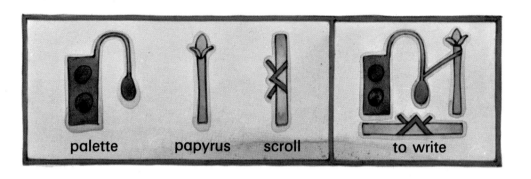

palette   papyrus   scroll   to write

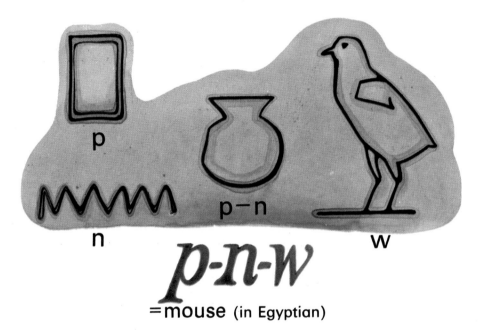

p

n

p-n

w

p-n-w

=mouse (in Egyptian)

Later, the Egyptians found new ways
of making words from pictures.
Here are two of them.
The bottom pictures are called hieroglyphs.
Hieroglyphs are pictures used to mean sounds.

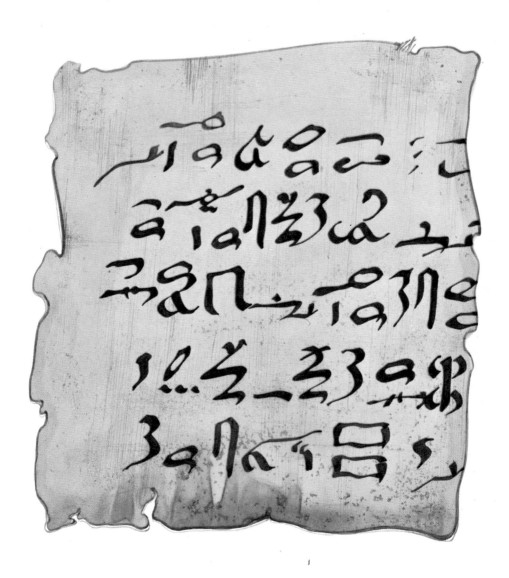

Here is some more Egyptian writing.
These pictures have become squiggles.
They could be written more quickly
than pictures.

12

Other people used Cuneiform writing.
This was made up of marks.
The marks were grouped
to make different patterns.
Each pattern stood for a sound.

13

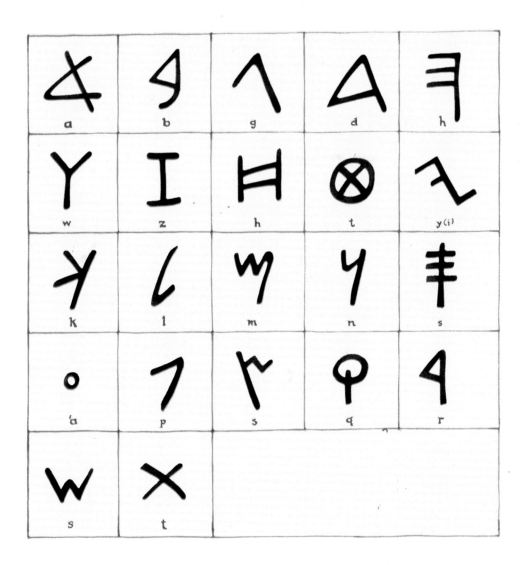

These letters were made by the Phoenicians.
The Phoenicians made the first alphabet.
It had 22 letters in it.

14

		gamal	g
		aleph	a
		heth	k
		daleth	d
		qoph	q

The letters began as pictures.
The picture of a camel meant 'camel'.
The Phoenicians called a camel a 'gamal'.
They began to use the camel sign
for the letter 'g'.

actor's mask

Here are some Greek actors.
One of them is reading his part.
The words are in Greek.
The Greeks used the Phoenician alphabet.
They changed some of the letters.
16

Here is some Roman writing.
The Roman alphabet came from the Greeks.
We use the Roman alphabet today.

Long ago, all books were written out by hand.
Monks copied out the books
on parchment paper.
They decorated the pages with pictures.

ECVN·DVM
ea quę in diuersis Libris Le
gimus Primus homo qui
se populauit in hispania
uocatus fuit Tubal a quo
processit natio iberorum

prout hoc testartur Isidorus et Ieronimus: et fuerut
uocati ex dicto nomine Tubal Cetubales: et exinde
a quadam stella uocata Hesperus quę circa solem
inter diem et noctem Lucet Terra illa fuit dicta
Hesperia: et dicti Cetubales popularunt se in riparia
iberis: et propter ipsam populationem dimisso nomi
ne de tubal sumpferunt nomen dicti fluminis quod

Here is a page written by a monk.
He used the Roman alphabet.
Monks often changed the shape of the letters.
The small letters were easier to write.

19

Rosetta Stone

The Rosetta Stone taught people
about some of the old alphabets.
Napoleon's soldiers found the Stone in Egypt.
20

Egyptian
hieroglyphic

Egyptian
Demotic

Greek

The Rosetta Stone had three kinds of writing.
They all said the same thing.
One of them was in Greek.
As people knew Greek, it helped them
to understand the other writings.

王看見龍

A King sees a Dragon

龍在山上

The Dragon is on a Mountain

Other people write in different directions.
Here is some Chinese writing.
It goes up and down the page.

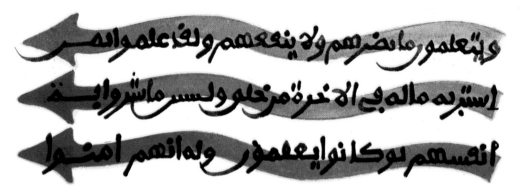

Hebrew

This is English
witten backwards

Greek
boustrophedon
writing

This is English
written in two
different directions

This picture shows Hebrew and Greek.
It shows how they would look in English.
Try reading the English in a mirror.
Hebrew looks backwards to us.
But to the Hebrews it does not look backwards.

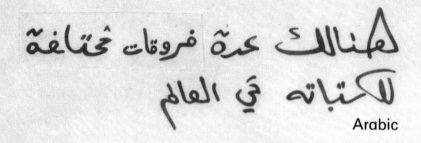

هنالك عدّة فروقات مُختلفة لكتابته في العالم

Arabic

There are many different kinds
of writing in the world.

Υπάρχουν πολλά διάφορα είδη γραψίματος εις τόν κόσμο.

Greek

We use the Roman alphabet.
It came from the Phoenician alphabet,
through the Greek.
So did many other alphabets.
Here are some of them.

В мире существует много различных алфавитов.

Russian

世界には たくさん の ちがった 文字が あります。

Japanese

עולם קיימות הרבה ידועות שונות של אותיות.

Hebrew

All these blocks of words
say the same thing.
But see how different they look
in different countries.

Pirates   sailed   to an island.

They   buried   treasure.

One man   drew   a map.

See if you can write your own picture messages.
Send them to your friends.

You could make your messages into a book.
Try making a folding book, like the Aztecs.

Index

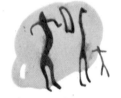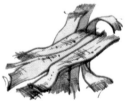